Another Step

is never too far

by

Mark Carter

I dedicate this book to my parents

Valerie and Michael Carter

" Mum you're my hero and always fought my corner"

"Dad you always inspired me to never quit and try harder"

I love you both dearly X X

Another Step Is Never Too Far

Mark Carter

Contents:

Chapter 1

"So, It Begins"

One

Whenever in life you decide to do something or recount an important "life event" the first question most people inevitably ask is where do I begin?
At the start seems to be the usual requisite response from many so that seems to me the best place to start my story. So, strap in and here goes.

Two

I hope you will enjoy my journey. My story begins as a small baby of six weeks old who was blessed to be adopted by Valerie and Michael Carter my parent's.
I have always referred to them as my parent's and have never looked for any of my biological family.

Three

I was blessed to be chosen by my parent's Valerie and Michael who had been told the very sad news they had a one in a million chance to have children of their own and this led to them being recommended to consider adopting a child and fortunately this was me. They went through a long process of assessments, interviews, references, and questions to get to the point they could adopt me. This proved a stressful time for them both. I will be forever grateful they persevered, and I am blessed to have them as my parent's.

Four

I was adopted on Michael's birthday 16th March 1972 and then my journey began. I put this down to sheer determination from Valerie and Michael and lots of hard work.
I think my determination to succeed in whatever I do certainly comes from them. They have both worked hard as well.

Five

Despite Mum and Dad's happiness over my adoption they still didn't give up the hope of Mum becoming pregnant, and it happened! Miraculously Mum fell pregnant and on 21 June 1975 my Mum gave birth to my brother

Christopher, approximately 2 years and 6 months after my adoption.

Six

I have been asked a few times over the years if I have ever wanted to track down my biological Mum or family and to be honest it has never really interested me, I can imagine the reasons why children are put up for adoption vary a lot and I guess I didn't really want to know as in Valerie and Michael I had two people willing to give me all their love, time and attention, and who gave me so much.

Seven

What made Valerie and Michael great parents? To be honest I don't think there is a specific reason that makes someone a great parent but for me my Mum and Dad gave me love, security, effort, and attention and I think that goes a very long way towards being a great parent, they also made sure I had opportunities to do whatever I wanted to in life, support is so important and I have always felt they've fully supported almost everything I have done.

Eight

So where was I born people ask? Well, I was born in Portsmouth in 1972 at St Mary's hospital and at 6 weeks old Valerie and Michael adopted me, so I never really grew up or got raised in Portsmouth, I have lived my entire life in Southampton and have never wanted to leave, I think the only other city I would have lived in would have been London as I enjoy how busy it is and in all honesty, there is so much to do and see there.

Nine

I was about 12 when my parent's told me they had adopted me, in all honesty I wasn't upset and it wasn't something that had a huge impact on me but I have always put that down to the fact that my parent's had treated me exactly the same as if I had been their biological Son so when they decided to tell me which I can imagine was not an easy decision to make or an easy discussion to have, I can imagine they were probably quite torn over how I would react to the news, however I have always said they are my parents so I didn't view them any differently as a result of my being adopted, if anything I've always been very grateful that they chose me.

Ten

So, did my adoption have any effect on me when Christopher my brother came along? Well in a nutshell the answer is no as I didn't know at the time of his birth that I was adopted, we did lots together as a family when we were both young and as a result there wasn't really an issue there, we have drifted apart over the years, but I think with some families' that sometimes happens.

Mum and Dad's career's

When Mum left school she did office work and worked at Cadena bakery, but Mum knew she wanted to be a nurse, despite leaving school without the necessary qualifications she managed to get a job as an auxiliary at the chest hospital on a children's ward.
She said this was the hardest job she had in nursing as she was seeing some young children who she had grown close to during caring for them being unwell and passing

away. Despite her not having the necessary qualifications she managed to get on a state enrolled nursing course because of a very kind matron. This proves that determination and hard work pay off.

Dad left school not sure what career path he would pursue, he was good at technical drawing and maths and his dad was in engineering, so I guess it was natural for Dad to follow his father's path and take an apprenticeship with Moorgreen Metals in Millbrook at the trading estate.

Mum trained as a nurse at Southampton General Hospital then spent several years at the Royal South Hants and then eye hospital. She spent her last ten years of her career as a community nurse which for Mum was the most rewarding.

Dad's career continued in engineering draughting and engineering project management continued and led to him working for Vosper Thorneycroft, Marshall Richards and British Gas.

When Dad reached 51 it proved to be a turning point in his career he took redundancy from British Gas and was hoping to work in the charity sector.

Dad was lucky enough to secure a job as a community fundraiser for the red cross which he found to be the most rewarding time in his career.

Chapter 2

"The Next Step"
One

I lived with my parents in Southampton in a lovely house in Sholing named " Bon Heur " French for " good hour " I grew up here and made my first friend's. Mum and Dad moved into this house in 1966 the year England won the World cup! I was schooled in my early years at Sunday School and started primary school at St Monica Infant's in Sholing Southampton in September 1977.

I had a great time at school and made a lot of friends many who I'm still friend's with to this day. Moving onto St Monica middle school in June 1983.

Two

I continued my education at St Monica Middle School and was lucky enough to attend a school trip to France we visited Le Havre and stayed at a school there, it was definitely an experience, my first time abroad, away from my home, a different country but I thoroughly enjoyed it and visited some wonderful places, Rouen, Honfleur, Etrata, Paris, learned about Joan of Arc, I also ate snails lol about 25 of them.

I appeared on Saturday Banana (a child's programme on ITV) whilst at St Monica Primary School and I met "Metal Mickey" the robot star of the show.

Three

Anyway, those were my earlier years, people often ask me how did I "become" disabled, I know some people do "become" disabled but I'm one of those who was born with it. I have Becker Muscular Dystrophy which I was diagnosed with age five, my diagnosis came about after a few occasions when I was around three years old when my parents noticed I got fatigued more than I should have and complained " my legs hurt " it turned out I was complaining because I kept getting cramp, my Mum was convinced something was wrong. She asked several people for help but was informed " there is nothing wrong with your son " however not convinced by this and knowing as a Mum something wasn't right, she continued to fight my cause and wanted to see a specialist and eventually her wish was granted, and we did. His verdict was the same as the GP. However Mum was still certain something was wrong and insisted on a second opinion. Eventually we were referred to a specialist from Southampton General Hospital, Professor Norman. We went to see him and after 10 minutes with him he had diagnosed me with Muscular Dystrophy subject to a biopsy.

After a muscle biopsy I was diagnosed with Muscular Dystrophy, initially this was Duchenne Muscular Dystrophy however it turned it to be Becker Muscular Dystrophy due to a misdiagnosis. So, we finally had an answer to why I was struggling. Despite my diagnosis my parent's endeavoured to give me all the opportunities any other child would have this included sport, clubs, holidays, and day's out. They also started a 40-year involvement with Southampton branch of Muscular Dystrophy, Dad went on to become

Chairman and Secretary and Mum Welfare Secretary. They were a huge help to me over the years and I am and will be forever grateful to the Muscular Dystrophy Association for all their support and grants I received over the years.

Four

I really enjoyed living at "Bon Heur" and we had some great friends who we played with and hung around with when we were there, we had a shop just around the corner and we all used to buy bottles of Corona soft drinks from there, and we always looked forward to returning them as at that time you got paid for returning them it wasn't a lot of money but we all liked 1p sweet's so it always went a long way.

Five

We were very lucky as behind where the houses in Pinegrove Road where we had an old quarry that had grown over with grass etc and we used to play there whenever we could, for boy's who loved Action Man toy's or Cowboy's and Indian's it was a great place to be able to go and play and we certainly made the most of our day's playing there.

Six

During the summer we were all hanging around each other's house's, riding our bike's and go karts around our area, we had a little sweet sale every now and then and they were just great times, we had an old air raid shelter behind where we lived that was made from concrete and had been there since the Second World War, it was a large structure and would always fill up with water, we always thought it would be an amazing "den" but to be honest we were only children and thankfully had parents who were sensible enough to ask us to stay clear of the shelter which we did.

Seven

I loved my time at St. Monica Primary and had a lovely teacher called Miss Treadgold, we used to do May Day dancing around a Maypole, we went to class in the same building that the Sunday school was held in and had some old Nissan hut's again left from the Second World War as Classroom's as well,

I always felt the corridor's at school were very cold but I always put it down to how long they were.

Eight

Sunday school was fun, although I don't really think I understood what it was all about, how many children understand what Sunday school or religion really is when they are younger. I guess learning about different things is sometimes confusing or hard to understand but also broadens your mind and helps you to be more open minded and understanding of others.

Nine

I started St Monica Primary in September 1977 and was there until moving to St Monica Middle in 1981 I was at St Monica Middle from 1981-1984 when I went up to Weston Park Boy's school (now Oasis Mayfield) I thoroughly enjoyed my school days at St Monica and the school disco's, nativity performance's TV appearance on Saturday Banana and meeting Bill Odie and Metal Mickey from the show. The school trip to Le Havre was a real highlight at

St Monica Middle, when I went to Weston Park I must admit my time there wasn't quite as nice as sadly I suffered bullying for the majority of my time there.

Ten

While I was at Weston Park, I took part in all games and P.E. lessons despite my physical limitations and did okay, I may not have been as fast or as strong as others but I always gave one hundred and ten percent and my games teacher Mr Bywater wrote in my school leavers report that despite not being as strong etcetera as others I always gave one hundred and ten percent and he knew of no greater trier.

It was while at Weston Park I started to play hockey and was reserve goalie for the school team, this opened the door to playing for Old Tauntonian's (now Southampton) I started with their colt's and later played for the otter's and 4th eleven and just broke into the 3rd eleven shortly before I stopped playing.

Chapter 3

" The Following Step "

One

My hockey playing days were enjoyable and I played between the ages of sixteen and twenty -four when I started working full time for Tesco and due to working weekends I couldn't play anymore.

Two

Mum and Dad moved to a bungalow in Caxton Avenue in Bitterne in 1978 because they thought I would be in a wheelchair by the time I was 10 or 11. Thankfully for us all due to the change in my diagnosis that didn't happen. I have always tried to live independently and never let my disability stand in my way, I always maintain there are many people far worse off than me, Sport was a huge part in my Dad's life and this rubbed off onto Mum and in turn myself and my Brother Christopher, I was always a Southampton FC supporter and despite my Muscular Dystrophy I played hockey in goal for Old Tauntonian's which Dad always thought it looked too dangerous!

Three

Chris played football for Itchen Tyro, won the

Southampton Schools table tennis twice and played badminton for Southampton Dad played league football and badminton when he joined British Gas and when he joined the badminton club at British Gas Mum also was able to join and play league.

Four

I was a cub scout with 14th Itchen South and went camping with them, I swam in gala's and won medals for it with the cubs I also starred in Roverang 1982 with the cub's, I joined 14th Itchen South scouts after cub's and continued to enjoy camping, hiking, I attended chief scout camp at Middle Wallop with 14th Itchen South. Whilst with 14th Itchen South I also climbed Pen-Y-Fan in the Brecon Beacons in Wales which is 2,907 feet above sea level. After 14th Itchen South I joined 3rd Itchen North Air scouts, and this is when my real passion for aircrafts was realised.

Five

I was lucky enough to have some amazing experiences through cub's and scout's, air scouts were a real great time in my life, I managed to win the "Champion's Trophy" with two other scouts from 3rd Itchen North.

Six

I flew a chipmunk trainer plane whilst with 3rd Itchen North air scout's and performed a loop and a barrel role, my first ever aerobatics' experience and needless to say I was quite green afterwards, also while with 3rd Itchen North air scout's I flew four seat tb nine light aircraft and was really lucky to fly in a Westland Wessex helicopter over Stonehenge.

Seven

I always had a passion for flying since the air scout's and one of my favourite movies about World War Two was " Reach for the Sky " the story of Sir Douglas Bader (pictured overleaf) who despite the loss of both his leg's in a flying accident went on to become a World War Two ace pilot during the Battle of Britain and the war.

Eight

Whilst looking around the internet one

afternoon researching where I could learn to fly, how to fly and where to fly I came across

an amazing organisation called " flying scholarships for the disabled" and " Aerobility" I applied for a scholarship and was fortunate to be selected twice by flying scholarships for the disabled to their final selection programme at RAF Cranwell, sadly on neither occasion was I successful.

Nine

I decided after leaving Cranwell to start learning to fly with Aerobility at Lasham near Basingstoke, I did 3 hour's training before I had an accident that prevented me from learning anymore, I did help Aerobility at an event they held at Sywell Aerodrome before I was forced to stop flying. My plan is to return to flying in the near future.

Ten

This section has been a fairly short one. I have rapidly approached my 50th birthday and God knows how I got this far lol! But it seems my recollection of dates is a little shaky at best (old age maybe!)

Chapter 4

"Love Of Football"

One

My Dad Michael being an avid Southampton fan made sure I grew up with a love for Southampton FC, I was four years old and watching Southampton FC in the 1976 FA Cup Final which we won, and I still vividly remember.

Two

What a day it was when the team came through Bitterne on their round city tour with the FA Cup, it was a scorching hot day and the excitement was tangible from everyone, what a day and what an occasion, a memory I shall never forget, and so my love of

Southampton FC began.

Three

My Dad Michael took me to my first game at "The Dell" in 1980 as Southampton took on a Vancouver Whitecaps team containing two players who featured for Saints during their careers. None other than Bruce Grobbelaar and Alan Ball.

Four

I continued attending with my Dad right through the eighties' and enjoyed what I believe to be one of the best Southampton team's I've been lucky enough to watch when we finished second to Liverpool in the 1983-84 season. We missed out on the title by just three points to Liverpool, I was also lucky to see Peter Shilton in his prime and Kevin Keegan.

Five

To this day I will never forget learning we had signed Keegan on Monday 11th February 1980 who at the time was European footballer of the year and two-time Ballon D'or winner! What a dream for a young fan! An unbelievable day that I still can't quite believe even now.

Six

None of us had any idea what was happening when Lawrie Mc Menemy called an unexpected press gathering at the Potter's Heron Hotel in Romsey, I don't know who was more stunned that day the press or the fans! Ha-ha! But an amazing moment I'll never forget.

Seven

So many great memories' I have of Southampton FC between 1980's -1990's and all thanks to my Dad, I will never be able to thank him enough. Little did I know that I would be lucky enough to see the debut of a mercurial young man from the Channel Islands in the form of one Matthew Le Tissier who made his debut in 1986.

Eight

I was lucky enough to see him illuminate everyone at Southampton with his skills and goal's, I am not sure if I will ever see another player that loyal or good in a Southampton shirt during my lifetime but what a treat it was to watch "Le God" as we all referred to him.

Nine

I was lucky enough to have a season ticket for the first five seasons at St Mary's after Southampton FC moved to their now home at St Mary's stadium, and I vividly remember the first game, me and Dad spent forty-five minutes' just in awe of our surroundings after the move from "The Dell" and totally forgot about the friendly we were watching.

Ten

The club eventually moved to a new home at St Mary's stadium in Southampton after leaving " The Dell" and despite some early struggles started winning at home, there were so many great games at St Mary's but I will always remember the 2003 season the most as we had an amazing cup run and I was at the final at the Millennium stadium in Cardiff, an amazing day out.

Chapter 5

" The Continuation "

One

After leaving Weston Park Boy's school in 1992 with 8 GCSE's I went in and out of work for several years until I worked for Tesco, this job with them lasted 5 years until at the age of 27 I was retired on the grounds of ill - health, however during my time with Tesco I was married and had children of my own.

Two

I had twin's, two boy's Scott and Macauly, they were born on 28th April 1996 and are both now 27 and have their own children, I don't talk about my marriage as it didn't end well, and I left the marital home when the boys were 5. To this day it will always be the hardest day I have ever experienced.

Three

After several years of not working and being "retired" I was fortunate to get involved with the S.D.S.A. Saint's Disabled Supporters'

Association and started volunteering with them after being co-opted onto the management committee I'm now in my third year with them.

Four

A lot of opportunities' have since come around because of my volunteering and it remains one of the best decision's I ever made and am grateful to Mark Harpur who was their Vice Chairman until very recently who originally suggested to the committee, I may be able to " bring something to the table "

Five

So, I spoke about the opportunities' I have had come my way because of my volunteering with the S.D.S.A so what were these opportunities'? Well, let's go through them, shall we? Yeah, why not! Lol.

Six

Every year the Saints' Disabled Supporters' Association hosts an open day at St Mary's this is designed to bring together the community, get children used to wheelchair user's and disabilities' and showcase accessibility and disability and local organisation's and demonstrate what the S D.S.A do. This event has a lot of Ex Saints who attend to give their support and sometimes even bring the odd item of memorabilia for us to sell to raise valuable funds. As a result of being at those events with the S.D.S.A. I have been fortunate enough to meet and chat with player's past and present which is a huge honour

Seven

I always thought I would like to give back and I feel being involved with the S.D.S.A has allowed me the opportunity to do that. It's good to feel I've been giving back to the community and helping others through my volunteering. This has definitely been a fulfilling experience, if you ever have a chance to volunteer then you totally should it has turned out to be just the best choice I ever made when I started.

Eight

Fundraising is a fundamental part of the work

the S.D.S.A. do and I always enjoy the collection's we do around the area of St Mary's stadium and the other things we do to raise money for our season tickets and open day. The open day and our season tickets bring such joy to other's and to know I contribute even if only in a small way makes me very proud to be involved.

Nine

I always thought it would be good to be able to help other's by working with or alongside Southampton FC and through the S.D.S.A I feel I can help to make a real difference for both able bodied and disabled fans alike at St Mary's and in the wider community

Ten

So, I was fortunate to be involved with grass roots football with Sholing FC for approximately two years, this came about after I was approached by Sholing FC Secretary, friend and radio presenter Greg Dickson who asked if I would consider becoming Pan Disability Secretary as the club felt that section needed more support, I agreed and following a club AGM I took up the post. I always wanted to be involved in disability football or grassroots or both and here was the opportunity, again this came about via community radio, and I will get to that later in the following pages. One of the first things that struck me is the skill level of Pan - Disability player's they are extremely good footballers despite any physical or other limitation's they are dealing with. Also, just the sheer determination and never give up attitude which I can totally relate to. I defy anyone to not be impressed by the effort, application, determination, and commitment Pan - Disability footballer's have.

Chapter 6

" Community Radio "

One

I now work on community radio voluntarily so how did I get that opportunity? I was initially invited onto a sport's program at Awaaz 99.8fm in Southampton called "Behind The Mic" to talk about the Saint's Disabled Supporters' Association and then got invited back on to join in with the show, I then became a permanent member of the show. I have now been on "Behind The Mic" for over three years now.

"The Dazey Hills Company"

While working with Awaaz, FM we had a visit from a local talent agency the Dazey Hills Company based in Southampton.
Who are the Dazey Hills company and what do they do? They are a talent agency and production company, they represent a very diverse range of actors, voice actors and production crew, but why were they at Awaaz FM?
Well, they came in to talk about themselves and what they do, and they also wanted to appeal for anyone who was disabled or had a disability to sign up with them as they wanted to promote actors with disabilities.

I contacted them as I was interested in acting and still am, they did contact me back and ask if I would like to join their list of talent, at the time this was a little difficult but at the time of writing I have decided to see if I can sign up with them and see where that may lead.

Two

I am pretty passionate about sport and the program is a great platform to talk about all sport's and offer my views and opinion on it. After some time, I thought it would be great to do a show of my own and asked if I could train to be a presenter.

It turned out that Awaaz FM had a sister station, Fiesta 95FM so after a little training I began a show on Fiesta with Mark Harpur who was also in the Saint's Disabled Supporters' Association, the show was named aptly " The Two Saint's Show " I thoroughly enjoyed the show and it was a real labour of love, getting to talk all things Southampton FC was awesome and myself and Mark bounced off of each other well and had a great banter on the show, we felt we should do a podcast version of the show and so we launched " The Two Saints Podcast Show" Mark's help was great during this time, he would compile the show and podcast running order and agenda's and I would take care of the technical stuff and any or all editing of the show and podcast.

Three

We did the podcast for approximately 2 years' but then as I had other commitment's and was struggling to dedicate the time and effort the show and podcast deserved, I decided we should stop both. This was a difficult decision at the time but one that it turned out was the correct one.

Four

How did I end up in a Coca Cola advert? This was an amazing experience and one I never in a million year's imagined would happen to me. The Saint's Disabled Supporters' Association were contacted by a talent agency who were looking to shoot an advert for a new Premier League campaign.

Five

The Premier League had struck a deal with Coca Cola for the 2019-20 league season and the talent agency had been tasked with finding disabled fans to participate in the advert as they wanted to make sure it was diverse and included real fans.

Six

So, Mark H and I volunteered and along with several other Southampton fans went to an old social club near Highbury to film for the day, we were offered a fee for taking apart along with a fuel allowance, the agency looked after us and provided refreshments.

Seven

I thought it would be fun to be involved and that's how it turned out. It was a long day but a fun one, we had to look like we were watching a Southampton game in the pub which was quite cool although me and Mark agreed it was freezing that day. Nevertheless, we did the filming and then travelled home, we thought we probably wouldn't be in the final cut of the advert, but it turned out we were.

Eight

I can now officially say I made it to the big screen as the advert I featured in was on in the cinema when Captain Marvel came out and in a re - edit I even had a line! It was a fun experience and one I will never forget and one I can definitely tell and show the grandkids about.

Nine

This only happened due to my volunteering work and I'm so grateful for the opportunities' this has given me as I never started volunteering to get anything in return, I just wanted to help other's.

Ten

I first got involved with Leonard Cheshire homes through the S.D.S.A doing a bucket collection with Leonard Cheshire homes in Romsey. Little did I realise Leonard Cheshire was one of the "Dambuster's" those daring aircrew's who delivered the "bouncing bomb" to a target during World War Two. He went on to care for a serviceman who had a few problems and from there Leonard Cheshire homes grew they now provide care and services to many people with many different needs. I met a lovely lady there by the name of Pat Moody, I have spoken with Pat a few times and we have agreed we will try to work together for the benefit of Leonard Cheshire and the S.D.S.A in the future, it was during one of these chats Trish said " you should write a book" so here I am! Thanks Trish!! Lol she knows I'm kidding. It was nice to be given a push in that direction as I've really enjoyed writing this book and it's taken me out of my comfort zone.

Chapter 7

" The Rozhi Saki Award "
One

What is the Rozhi Saki award? The Rozhi Saki award was created by Awaaz FM to pay tribute to their former director Rozhi who sadly passed away, she was very passionate about Awaaz FM and the award is given out to presenter's who have gone above and beyond whilst working at the station

Myself & Greg Dickson with our Rozhi awards

Two

I sadly never met Rozhi but I am sure I would of got on with her very well as I tend to get on with most people I meet and she was clearly passionate about Awaaz FM as I am so I think it would of been a pleasure and honour to work alongside her.

Three

I was lucky enough along with Sunny Aheer another of Awaaz FM's great presenter's to be nominated for this award in 2019 and we were both awarded the certificates for our award by the Mayor of Southampton, also we were sent on an all-expenses paid mini cruise and a lunch on the Isle of Wight.

Four

An opportunity came along for a Drive Time presenter on Awaaz FM and I asked if I could train for the role, following three weeks of training with one of our other Drive Time presenter's, Barry Barnett and our boss Ali Beg I was given the Thursday Drive Time show 4-6pm on Awaaz 99.8fm the show goes out across Hampshire, online globally and in Birmingham on FM and DAB. I really enjoy presenting the show and we have an amazing bunch of presenter's working there. I can honestly say it's the nicest environment I have ever worked in. Plus also now I do Wednesday's Show as well.

Five

The best part about the show's on Awaaz FM and Fiesta FM that I do are I can do something for the community, I can give back to the community and I enjoy doing them, also I get to do interview's and invite guests onto my shows.

Six

I do Behind The Mic every Monday one to three pm on both station's as we stream across both, I really enjoy Behind The Mic as we discuss all sport worldwide and offer our view's and opinion and as I'm passionate about sport it's a perfect show for me.

Seven

Fiesta Sizzler's I do every Saturday eight to nine pm is an hour of club classic's, I record this at home for it to go out each week, I enjoy this show as it's more music than chat and it's nice to be a bit more diverse.

Eight

Fiesta 95 football special I do this on a Thursday from 1pm, I talk facts and figures about the world's greatest footballer's and their lives' and career's and play music from the most successful time of their career. It's good to be able to add something different to Fiesta FM as it's a Latin station.

Nine

Drivetime, I do on Awaaz FM every Wednesday & Thursday 4-6pm and this goes out on FM, DAB and globally and via Facebook live, I enjoy the show as I deliver weather and travel bulletin's, music from the two thousand's till now, have feature's included and get to do interviews in the studio and via zoom.

Ten

The best part about all the radio work I now do is that I have upskilled I have gone from just being a show guest to a presenter but am now also able to create and edit my own podcast if need be and my own playlist's and promo's and jingle's if I need any. I never imagined when I started on radio how far I would get with it, and to win an award for it and be recognised by the Mayor of Southampton was an amazing honour I will remember forever.

Chapter 8

"Things I've Done and Achieved"

One

I did quite a lot while I was with the cub's and scouts over the year's and always enjoyed camping, hiking, swimming. I won medals in cub and scout swimming gala's two golds in fact. I attended chief scout camp at Middle Wallop which was amazing, these camps are a gathering of troop's from all over, it's known now as a jamboree.

Two

Fernycroft's is well known for cub and scout camping but sadly for me my first scout stays there resulted in a very nasty case of nettle rash and our leader spent most of my time camping treating me with camomile lotion to stop the horrible itching and how tight the rash made my skin.

Three

Bob a job week was always interesting, we basically did things like shoeshine's, making tea, clearing leave's, all to raise money but also to help the community in some small way, I turned out to be a pretty good tea maker lol.

Four

I always looked forward to cubs as Dad used to buy me chips on the way home which was always a treat to look forward to. The scout hut was in Spring Road and when I moved up to scout's we had access to a " tuck shop " here we could buy drink's, crisp's, and sweet's which we all consumed fairly heavily ha-ha.

Five

When I moved up to scout's it took a while to get used to the fact that the leaders were all named as characters from the jungle book, Akela, Baloo, Bagheera etcetera but it was also kind of cool, scouts were a big difference from cub's as it was more physical in my view and included things like, rock climbing, kayaking, hiking, abseiling.

Six

We attended church services as cub's and scout's, we would march to them bearing our troop flag, these were always Remembrance Service's and it was a big honour to be the flag bearer, I was lucky enough to be given that opportunity once which I enjoyed, although it's surprising how heavy the flag and pole is.

Seven

I think my best moment with scout's was staying in the Brecon Beacon's, we camped in a place called Abergavenny it was a lovely little town, the field we camped in had a river at the bottom that we swam in, and rock jumped at, the village itself reminded me of Cornwall a little but was a very picturesque place to stay.

Eight

Whilst we were in Abergavenny we were fortunate enough to take a trip to Snowdonia and did a hike to and up Pen - Y - Fan which is two thousand nine hundred and seven feet above sea level, I absolutely loved this and although for me I found it slightly more difficult than other's I relished the challenge, this would also turn out to be when I discovered the wonders of Kendal Mint cake which I still eat to this day.

Nine

Pen y Fan is the highest peak in South Wales, situated in the Brecon Beacon's. At eight hundred and eighty-six metre's it is also the highest British peak south of Cadair Idris in Snowdonia. It is the highest point of the historic county of Brecknockshire. The twin summits of Pen y Fan at two thousand nine hundred and seven feet and Corn Dua at two thousand eight hundred and sixty-four feet were formerly referred to as Cadair Arthur or 'Arthur's Seat'.

Ten

One of the best parts of the hike up Pen -Y-Fan apart from the scenery was the feeling of accomplishment and I was totally euphoric as for me I saw this as a massive milestone in my life. It was literally "reaching the summit" at the time of everything I managed to accomplish despite my physical limitations. The scenery from the summit and in the surrounding areas is the most beautiful I've seen I feel blessed to of been able to see this for myself, it does give you a new perspective on things for sure. We were also lucky enough that two tornado fighter jets flew past while we were at the summit. They were actually below us as they passed as they were low level training in the valley's but what a sound and what a sight, I absolutely loved it.

" The broken leg "

7 years ago, August 2015 can definitely say was one of the worst things I ever went through, I had agreed to do a challenge and, on my way, slipped on a wet floor and snapped my left femur, I have never felt that much pain or sounded so much like Chewbacca from Star Wars! Ha ha! I literally sounded like him every time I shouted in pain, the worst part aside from the pain was laying immobile on a freezing cold tiled floor waiting for the paramedics.

When they did arrive and after assessing me gave me morphine and gas and air it was a relief although it didn't fully remove all the pain.

When I reached the hospital I was put into traction to help re - align the thigh bone and this relieved a fair bit of pain combined with the morphine etcetera I was given.

The next stage was the operation to fix the broken bone, this involved inserting a titanium rod from hip to knee through the centre of my femur and then two screws inserted in the knee and hip ends to secure the rod.

Without this procedure I think me ever walking again at all with my muscular dystrophy would have been a tall order maybe 20 odd years ago, however this operation proved successful and I was stunned the next day when the physio's arrived with a walker frame and said right we are going to get you on your feet. I was gobsmacked I'd only broken the bone two days before!

So, the process of my rehabilitation had begun and i was very surprised they wanted me up so quickly! So here I was now part cyborg Ha! Ha! and learning to walk again. I must admit the equipment they used was a big help. The first piece of equipment was brought in the morning after my operation, and the plan was to get me up and touch toe weight bearing, so tip toes and about twenty five percent bodyweight, this was a scary moment, but it went well and afterwards the plan was to do an Xray and see how everything was looking.

The Xray results came back and all was well so the plan moving forward was to increase the amount of weight bearing as I went on, so the next step after a few days was to do fifty percent which also went well I felt like I was making good progress but also worried I was doing too much but the physios and everyone looking after me convinced me it was all very good.

I spent about a week in Southampton General

hospital and then transferred to the Royal South Hants hospital to continue my rehabilitation, the reason for this was to ensure I had daily physio and continued my recovery.

I must admit the nurse's and physio's and all the staff were superb, a lovely bunch who really looked after me, the physios were amazing and I grateful to them all, and the food well what a difference from the general hospital.

All in all, I was in hospital for eight weeks, one week at Southampton general and seven at the Royal South Hants.

The day came for me to go home and by this stage I was almost putting full weight on my leg but was sent home with a gutter frame and continued my re-hab at home.

Everything went well until I began walking with crutches, I had been on anti - clotting medication while in hospital but this was stopped on my going home.

I had been walking with crutches for a few days and then my leg had swollen to about three times its size and was really stiff, I contacted the physio who advised we would get a doctor to come have a look, the doctor did and immediately sent me to hospital for a scan, it turned out I had three blood clots in the previously broken leg. It turned out we were lucky we caught them in time. One was near my ankle, another behind my knee and the third in my groin. So, it was then six months on blood thinners to treat the clots which touch wood have not returned since. All in all, my full recovery took about a year and a half, but it did turn out I was okay, so I am grateful for the fact I was treated so swiftly and looked after so well.

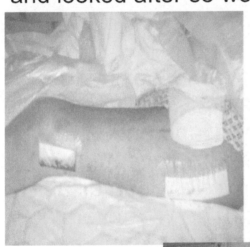 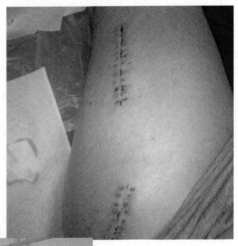

Chapter 9

" Inspiration "

One

Why did I decide to write a book people have and will ask me, the simple answer is a good friend of mine said "you should write a book" as we had spoken a few times and had shared stories' about our lives', so thank you to Pat Moody for the idea!

Two

What is my aim and what am I looking to achieve from writing this book, well the simple answer is I would like to try and encourage and inspire other people who have muscle wasting condition's or anyone with a disability to show them that you can do whatever you want in life with a positive outlook and a positive mind?

Three

Who are my inspirations in life? There are and have been a few. My Mum who always fought hard for me to get me the support and help I would need, my Dad for his hard work and volunteer work and always treating me as his own.

Four

I am inspired by both of my parent's for always supporting me no matter what and for giving me every possible chance they could. There are people I have met throughout my life but those who inspire me most are always those with disabilities' as I can relate to them, and I love to see people who have disabilities' showing what they're capable of.

Five

People I've met who inspire me are, Hamble Club Youth FC Pan - Disability, Sholing FC Pan - Disability which I was Secretary of for a while, Solent Boccia team, Aaron Phipps and people I meet with physical and mental disabilities.

Six

Other people I'm inspired by include, Sir Douglas Bader, Leonard Cheshire, Amelia Earhart, and Warwick Davis. These people for me are all about challenging stereotype's, conquering challenges, and succeeding against the odds.

Seven

Why does Sir Douglas Bader inspire me? Here are why, just a few facts about him.

Sir Douglas Bader

Nickname: Dogsbody

Born 21 February 1910

Died 5 September 1982 (aged 72)

 Royal Air Force Years of service: 1928 to 1933 and 1939 to 1946

Rank: Group Captain

Commands held: Tangmere Wing, Duxford Wing No. 242 Squadron

Second World War: Battle of France, Battle of Dunkirk, Operation Dynamo, Battle of Britain Adlertag, The Hardest Day Battle of Britain Day The Blitz

Awards: Knight Bachelor

Commander of the Order of the British Empire

Distinguished Service Order & Bar

Distinguished Flying Cross & Bar

Aviation consultant

Disabled activist

Eight

He joined the RAF in 1928 and was commissioned in 1930. In 1931, while attempting some aerobatics', he crashed and lost both his leg's. Having been on the brink of death, he made a recovery, then retook flight training, and passed his check flight's and then requested reactivation as a pilot. Although there were no regulation's applicable to his situation, he was retired against his wishes on medical ground's. After the outbreak of the Second World War Douglas Bader
returned to the RAF and was accepted as a pilot. He took part in the Battle of Britain after he scored his first victories over Dunkirk during the Battle of France in 1940. He went on to become a friend of Air Vice Marshal

Trafford Leigh-Mallory and his "Big Wing" experiments.

Nine

In August 1941, he baled out over German-occupied France and was captured. During this time, he met and was befriended by Adolf Galland, a prominent German fighter ace. Despite his disability, he made a number of escape attempt's and was eventually sent to Colditz Castle. He remained there until April 1945 when the camp was liberated by the First United States Army.

Ten

Bader left the RAF permanently in February 1946 and resumed his career in the oil industry. During the 1950's a book and a film "Reach for the Sky" all about his life and RAF career to the end of the Second World War were released.
He campaigned for the disabled and in the Queen's Birthday Honour's 1976 was appointed a Knight Bachelor for service's to disabled people. He continued to fly until his health forced him to stop in 1979. He died,

aged 72, on 5 September 1982 after a heart attack.

Eleven

Why am I inspired by Leonard Cheshire?
Here's a brief run down about him.
The Lord Cheshire Wing Commander in January 1943
Born 7 September 1917 - Died 31 July 1992
Place of rest Cavendish Cemetery
Royal Air Force Years of service: 1937 to 1946
102 Squadron RAF No. 35
Squadron RAF Commands held: No. 617
Squadron RAFÂ (1943 to 1944) RAF Marston Moor (1943) No. 76 Squadron RAFÂ (1942 to 43)
Second World War Awards: Victoria Cross
Member of the Order of Merit, Distinguished Service Order &Two Bars, Distinguished Flying Cross
Wives: Constance Binney (1941 to 1951), Sue Ryder (1959 to 1992)
Relations Geoffrey Chevalier Cheshire (father)

Twelve

Among the honour's he received as a pilot was the Victoria Cross, the highest award for gallantry in the face of the enemy that can be awarded to British and Commonwealth forces. He was the youngest group captain in the RAF and one of the most highly decorated pilots of the war. After the war he founded a hospice that grew into the charity Leonard Cheshire Disability. He became known for his work in resolving conflicts. In 1991 he was made a life peer in recognition of his charity work.

Thirteen

Amelia Earhart inspires me due to her aviation feats. Here is a breakdown of why she inspires me. Amelia Mary Earhart was an American aviation pioneer and author. Earhart was the first female aviator to fly solo across the Atlantic Ocean. She set many other record's, was one of the first aviators to promote commercial air travel, wrote books about her flying experiences, and was instrumental in the formation of The Ninety-Nine's, an organization for female pilot's.
Born: Amelia Mary Earhart July 24, 1897, In Atchison, Kansas, U.S.
Disappeared July 2, 1937 (aged 39) over the Pacific Ocean, on route to Howland Island from Lae, New Guinea

Declared dead in absence January 5, 1939 (aged 41)
Other names known by: Lady Lindy (after Charles Lindbergh) Meeley (childhood)
Alma mater Ogontz School Columbia University

Fourteen

Known for many early aviation records, including first woman to fly solo across the Atlantic Ocean
Husband George P. Putnam 1931
She was Born and raised in Atchison, Kansas, and later in Des Moines, Iowa and developed a passion for adventure at a young age, steadily gaining flying experience in her twenties'. Earhart became the first female passenger in 1928 to cross the Atlantic by airplane for which she achieved celebrity status. In 1932, piloting a Lockheed Vega 5B, Earhart made a nonstop
solo transatlantic flight, becoming the first woman to achieve this milestone. She received the United States Distinguished Flying Cross for this accomplishment.

Fifteen

In 1935, Earhart became a visiting faculty member at Purdue University as an advisor to aeronautical engineering and a career counsellor to women students. She was also a member of the National Woman's Party and an early supporter of the Equal Right's Amendment.

Sixteen

She is known and was known as one of the most inspirational American figures in aviation from the late 1920's throughout the 1930's, and her legacy is often compared to the early aeronautical career of pioneer aviator Charles Lindbergh, as well as to figures like First Lady Eleanor Roosevelt for their close friendship and lasting impact on the issue of women's causes from that period. During an attempt at becoming the first female to complete a circumnavigational flight of the globe in 1937 in a Purdue-funded Lockheed Model 10-E Electra, she, and her navigator Fred Noonan disappeared over the central Pacific Ocean near Howland Island. The two were last seen in Lae, New Guinea, on July 2, 1937, on the last land stop before Howland Island and one of their final legs of the flight.

Seventeen

She presumably lost her life in the Pacific during the circumnavigation, just three weeks prior to her fortieth birthday. Nearly one year and six months after she and Noonan disappeared, she was officially declared dead in her absence. investigations and significant public interest in their disappearance still continue over eighty years later. 15 Decade's after her presumed death, she was inducted into the National Aviation Hall of Fame in 1968 and the National Women's Hall of Fame in 1973. She now has several commemorative memorials named in her honour around the United States, including an urban park, an airport, a residence hall, a museum, a research foundation, a bridge, a cargo ship, an earth-fill dam, four schools, a hotel, a playhouse, a library, multiple roads, and more. She also has a minor planet, planetary corona and newly- discovered lunar crater named after her. She is ranked ninth on Flying's list of the fifty-one Heroes of Aviation.

Eighteen

I'm also inspired by Warwick Davis as he has

dealt with a disability his entire life, so here is some information on Warwick and his amazing life and career.

Warwick Ashley Davis English actor, comedian, filmmaker, and television presenter.

He played the lead character in Willow and the Leprechaun films, several characters in the Star Wars film series, most prominently the Ewok Wicket, and Professor Filius Flitwick and Griphook in the Harry Potter film series.

Davis starred as a fictionalised version of himself in the sitcom Life's Too Short. He has also presented the ITV game show's Celebrity Square's and Tenable from 2016 until the present time.

He was born Warwick Ashley Davis on 3 February 1970 in Epsom, Surrey, England

Year's actively working: 1982 to present

Height 3 ft 6 in

Wife: Samantha Burroughs (m.1991)

Children 4, including Annabelle Davis

Relative's: Peter Burroughs (father-in-law)

Website: warwickdavis.co.uk.

Active within the industry since he was twelve, Davis is the highest grossing supporting actor of all time (not including cameo's), owing mainly to his appearances in the Star War's and Harry Potter series of films.

Nineteen

Aaron Phipps is another inspiration, and his story is quite remarkable and I really admire his attitude, here is a brief rundown about him. Aaron Phipps is a British wheelchair rugby player and gold medal winning Paralympian.
Birth name: Aaron Phipps
Date of birth: 7 April 1983
Place of birth: Southampton
Wife; Vicky Phipps
Children: 2 daughters'

Twenty

Aaron is part of the Great Britain national wheelchair rugby team and competed in Wheelchair rugby at the 2012 Summer Paralympics' in London, And in Wheelchair rugby at the 2020 Summer Paralympics' where the team won the final on the 29th August 2021 and received gold medals.

Twenty-One

On 7 January 1999 he contracted Meningitis

C and Meningococcal sepsis. As a result of this illness, he was in a controlled coma for two weeks. Following this, in March, it was required that his legs and most of his fingers be amputated. In total he spent a year in hospital, receiving treatment and recovering. In 2007 he got involved in wheelchair race's and raised money for a Meningitis charity by completing a 10 km race in Totton. He has also completed 2 London Marathon's (2008 & 2009) and in 2009 was ranked 4th UK Male in both the London Marathon and the Adidas Silverstone Half Marathon.

Twenty-Two

On 23 May 2016 Aaron became the first disabled Brit to scale Mount Kilimanjaro during large parts of the ascent he was forced to climb on his hands and knees because the wheelchair wasn't capable of moving through the difficult terrain, but he was able to complete the climb without any assistance. He was told that he had to be carried up the mountain, however he refused to give up or accept the suggestion. When climbing the mountain, it took twice the time it was predicted to take. On the third day, the wheelchair wasn't capable of moving up the mountain anymore and so Aaron decided to use his knee pads in order to be able to reach the summit, with his father carrying the wheelchair.

Twenty-Three

I was lucky enough to speak with Aaron on the Behind The Mic sports show I do on Awaaz FM with Greg Dickson and Aaron's positive attitude was infectious and his story is totally inspiring, and better still he is a Sotonian!! Awesome. So, these are people who have inspired me in my life so far. And I think it's fair to say they all demonstrate a never give up on anything mindset which is one I like to believe I have managed to instil in myself.

Picture overleaf
L to R: Greg Dickson Aaron Phipps & Mark Carter.

Twenty-Four

I've been quite fortunate over the years to have met some amazing people and experience some amazing thing's and had some amazing opportunities' and I'm so grateful for all of them.

Chapter 10

" I Met Who!! "

One

I've been fairly lucky over the years to meet some great people, these are the people I've been fortunate enough to meet, ex Southampton players Matt le Tissier and Franny Benali, Southampton FC captain James Ward - Prowse, Southampton FC manager Ralph Hassenhuttl, Bruce Dickinson (lead singer Iron Maiden), former Southampton player's Nick Holmes, Reuben Agboola, Jim Steele, Peter Rodrigues, former Southampton manager's Dave Merrington and Lawrie Mc Menemy, and Dame Jenny Murray (BBC tv presenter).

Two

A lot of people, and I don't like to name drop but the reason for mentioning them all is this has all come about from volunteering and wanting to do good thing's within the community. If I hadn't started volunteering I may not of met half the people I have been lucky enough to.

Three

All the ex-Southampton players and the two former managers I have met at an annual event held by the Saint's Disabled Supporters' Association usually held at St Mary's stadium in the Kingsland concourse every August, it is a great day out and it is a great chance to meet player's past and present and see what accessibility at the stadium is like and a showcase of organisation's and sport's that benefit disabled fans.

Four

Dame Jennifer Susan Murray is a journalist, and tv presenter, she presented South Today in the seventies and early eighties, I met Dame Jenny when I was a young boy, I was at a Muscular Dystrophy Association summer.

fete and Dame Jenny opened the fete, I was tasked with going on stage to present her with some flowers as a thank you.

Five

I met Bruce Dickinson at RAF Cranwell, Bruce is the lead singer and frontman of Iron Maiden my favourite group, the reason I was at Cranwell was I had applied to "flying scholarships for the disabled" for a scholarship to learn to fly Bruce had been invited along as a guest, we were at Cranwell for three days and on the second day were told we would have a guest making an appearance.

Six

I was really intrigued as to who it would be as I think all of us were who attended, so we were all gathered in the bar area at Cranwell and the double door's swung open and there in front of us beer in hand, England rugby shirt on was none other than Bruce Dickinson of Iron Maiden.

Seven

Bruce is a qualified commercial pilot and fly's the Iron Maiden jet when the band tour, the jet is given Iron Maiden livery for the duration of the tour and when the tour ends the aircraft is returned to its usual commercial livery.

Eight

He told us a few stories' and some anecdote's and I was riveted listening to his tales of how he became a pilot what inspired him to start and some of the amusing things that happened when flying.

Nine

For me it was a great day, my favourite group's lead singer was in my presence telling us all how he became a pilot, what started the journey, flying the Iron Maiden jet, being a commercial pilot, the fact he was there had inspired me already.

Ten

Whilst I was at Cranwell I had to have an interview in front of the selection panel and sat in the front row was Bruce himself. As I spoke about why I wanted to fly and my experience's and flying using a hand rudder he paid full attention to everything I said, I must admit I've never been so nervous! Lol. Sadly, I didn't get a scholarship, but I had met an idol, so I was pretty chuffed, what made it even better was Bruce agreeing to a photo with me.

Chapter 11

" What is Muscular Dystrophy"

One

I'm hoping this chapter will give people a better understanding of Duchenne and Becker Muscular Dystrophy so here are some details of both forms of the genetic disease. I suffer from Becker Muscular Dystrophy.

Two

Duchenne Muscular Dystrophy is a severe, progressive, muscle-wasting disease that leads to difficulties with movement and, eventually, to the need for assisted ventilation and premature death. The disease is caused by mutations in encoding dystrophin that prevent the production of any dystrophin in muscle. Muscles without dystrophin are more sensitive to damage, resulting in progressive loss of muscle tissue and function, in addition to cardiomyopathy.

Three

Recent studies' have greatly deepened understanding of the primary and secondary genetic mechanisms. A number of therapies' that aim to restore the missing dystrophin protein or address secondary pathology have received regulatory approval and many others are in clinical development.

Four

Becker Muscular Dystrophy which I suffer from is a genetic disorder that gradually makes the body's muscle's weaker and smaller. It causes less severe problems than the most common type, Duchenne Muscular Dystrophy. Becker MD symptoms can range from mild to almost as severe as the symptoms of Duchenne MD.

Five

A child with Becker MD may start to walk later than most kid's do. But the disease rarely causes health problems until a child has muscle weakness in the hips and pelvis. This usually happens when kids are ten to thirteen years' old. Walking problems are usually noticed around age fifteen and sixteen. A child with Becker MD may have more difficulty with sport's, have trouble climbing stairs, not be able to walk quickly, run smoothly, or maintain a running pace, have trouble lifting heavy loads have calf muscles that look bigger than normal, even though they're weaker.

Six

Becker MD affects the muscles of the hip's, pelvis, thighs, and shoulders, as well as the heart. Changes in the heart muscle may happen faster than in other muscles. Children who first show symptoms of Becker MD at younger ages are more likely to have heart problems than kid's whose symptom's start later. Becker MD is progressive, meaning problem's get worse with age. Symptom's get worse slowly compared with Duchenne MD. Breathing muscles tend to stay strong enough that a ventilator or other mechanical breathing help isn't needed.

Seven

In Becker MD, muscles weaken because dystrophin, a protein made by muscle cell's, doesn't work as it should. A change in the dystrophin gene makes the protein too short. The flawed dystrophin puts muscle cells at risk for damage with normal use. Usually, the body will repair or replace damaged muscle cells. But in Becker MD, the cell's die instead. After the muscle cells die, they are replaced by fat and scar tissue.

Eight

Among children with the Becker MD gene, boys are most affected with weakness in their arm and leg movements. That's because the dystrophin gene is on the X chromosome. Boys have only one X chromosome, but girls have two. So, girl's almost always have a second copy of the gene that can make the full, working dystrophin protein. Girls can be carrier's and are at risk of passing this on to their children. Girls can also have symptoms, but in general they are less severe than in boys.

Nine

Both boys and girls with a Becker MD gene can have heart problems. Most children with a faulty dystrophin gene get it from the Mother, who may carry the faulty gene without knowing it. In some children, the faulty gene is a new genetic change called a mutation or variation. Doctors often diagnose muscular dystrophy based on the child's family history, symptom's, and an exam. These tests confirm the diagnosis and determine the type of muscular dystrophy:

Ten

Creatine Kinase level: This blood test checks the level of creatine kinase, a protein that normally stays inside muscle cells. When muscular dystrophy damages muscle cell's, they release CK into the blood.
Muscle biopsy: This test can show whether the

muscle has any dystrophin. If there's no dystrophin around the muscle fibres, it usually means the child has Duchenne MD. Patchy, reduced amounts of dystrophin around the muscle fibre's usually mean the child has Becker MD. The doctor does the biopsy by removing a small piece of muscle, usually from the thigh.

Genetic testing: This will show if there is a missing piece (deletion), duplication, or a point mutation in the dystrophin gene, which disrupts how the gene works. This helps the medical team decide how to treat the problem and know what to expect in the future.

Eleven

There's no cure yet for Becker MD. Treatment is a combination of slowing the disease and assisting the heart using medicine's helping the child move around using braces and other physical aids. A child with Becker MD usually is cared for by a team of doctors and other experts from several paediatric specialties. Kids with Becker MD can live long, active lives', and research to improve treatment is underway. Some people with Becker MD begin using a wheelchair in their twenties'. But many over age fifty can walk without help or by using a cane, crutches', or walker. Becker MD does not affect muscles of the bowel and bladder or sexual function. If the mother and any sisters of a child with Becker MD are found to be a carrier, they should have regular visits with a cardiologist (a doctor who specializes in heart problems).

Twelve

Children with Muscular Dystrophy may have a harmful response to anaesthesia. If your child must have surgery, make sure the anaesthesiologist is aware of the MD. Genetic counselling should be a consideration for any adult with a Becker MD gene before having children.

Chapter 12

" Epilogue"

One

So, what comes next who knows!! But it has been a great ride through life and as I reached 50 on January 30th, 2022! If the second half century is as good as the first, then my story has been a great one! The aim of this book and my aim in life I guess it would be fair to say is to hopefully inspire my family, my grandchildren and others to never give up on your dreams and never say " I can't do that " because as the title of this book says, " another step is never too far".

Two

Thank you so much to everyone who has helped me on my journey through life and inspired me and inspired my book and contributed to my book and life journey I am forever grateful. Also, a huge thank you to every single person I have met along the way who has helped me achieve what I have.

Three

To my grandchildren, always chase your dreams, be positive, you can do anything you want in life as long as you try. I am very proud of you all and I hope in some small way I can and will inspire you to be the best that you can be.

Four

I wonder what the next Fifty years will bring. Who knows but as the lyrics of a well-known song go, "life's a rollercoaster, just gotta ride it" I look forward to the next half century to see where my journey continues and watching my grandchildren grow and blossom and learn?

Five

I hope you have enjoyed reading my story of my journey, I hope this will inspire you and others to follow your dreams and always try to do whatever you wish to in life, a positive attitude can help so much, nothing is beyond reach if you try hard. I hope my story and my journey will also inspire my grandchildren and give lots more people a better understanding of disability and how it can affect people but also to show that disability doesn't have to stop you.

The

key

part

about

disability

is

the

word

"ability".

A tribute to Valerie my Mum

I'm including this section into the book as sadly since I wrote the first draft my Mum passed away following a battle with dementia.

My Mum was always so determined in life and so positive in whatever she did, I remember my Dad telling me how determined Mum was when he reminisced about her pushing him off his bike on his way home on one occasion to get his attention and making it very clear she wanted him to commit to her which he duly did,

It was the same when Mum decided she wanted to be a nurse she did not have the qualifications to get on the state nursing scheme but while working as an auxiliary a matron at Mum's workplace persuaded those in charge of the state scheme that they needed to get her on the scheme.

That was the beginning of Mum's long career in nursing, she went on to work at the children's chest hospital, Royal South Hants, Southampton General Hospital and Southampton eye hospital then also went on to do Macmillan cancer care, nurse at GP surgery and district nurse.

I like to think my positivity and sheer determination come from Mum as she was the most determined positive person I know.

She was an amazing Grandparent and almost second Mum to my two boys Scott and Macaulay who she had every weekend along with my Dad.

Another step is never too far and this journey that I have been on so far is dedicated to everyone who have made my step closer.
Without your support my journey would probably have been impossible but the thing with a disability is all about ability.

My ability has been to put pen to paper so to speak and hopefully my journey will inspire others to achieve what they feel is at times an impossibility.

Achieve your aspirations no matter what life put's in your way to make your goal's come true.

Mark Carter ©